50 German Lunch Recipes for Home

By: Kelly Johnson

Table of Contents

- Schnitzel with Potato Salad
- Beef Rouladen with Red Cabbage and Spaetzle
- Goulash with Bread Dumplings
- Currywurst with Fries
- Jägerschnitzel with Mushroom Gravy and Mashed Potatoes
- Lentil Soup with Frankfurters
- Königsberger Klopse (Meatballs in Caper Sauce) with Boiled Potatoes
- Sauerbraten with Potato Dumplings and Red Cabbage
- Kasseler Ripchen with Sauerkraut and Mash
- Leberkäse with Fried Eggs and Potato Salad
- Maultaschen (Swabian Ravioli) with Salad
- Labskaus (Corned Beef Hash) with Fried Egg and Pickles
- Grünkohl (Kale) with Pinkel Sausage and Boiled Potatoes
- Bratwurst with Sauerkraut and Mustard
- Beef Rouladen with Potato Dumplings and Green Beans
- Senfeier (Mustard Eggs) with Potatoes
- Labskaus with Rollmops and Pickled Onions
- Flammkuchen (German Pizza) with Salad
- Wurstsalat (Sausage Salad) with Bread
- Käsespätzle (Cheese Spaetzle) with Fried Onions
- Hackbraten (German Meatloaf) with Potato Salad
- Sülze (Head Cheese) with Potato Salad and Pickles
- Linseneintopf (Lentil Stew) with Sausage
- Frikadellen (German Meatballs) with Potato Salad
- Käsesuppe (Cheese Soup) with Pretzel Rolls
- Schweinshaxe (Pork Knuckle) with Sauerkraut and Bread Dumplings
- Käsespätzle with Caramelized Onions and Salad
- Erbsensuppe (Pea Soup) with Wiener Wurstchen
- Gulaschsuppe (Goulash Soup) with Bread
- Wurstsalat with German Bread
- Bauernfrühstück (German Farmer's Breakfast) with Bread
- Kartoffelsuppe (Potato Soup) with Croutons
- Käsefondue (Cheese Fondue) with Bread and Pickles
- Bratwurst with Potato Salad and Mustard
- Labskaus with Fried Egg and Pickled Herring

- Grünkohl with Mettwurst and Boiled Potatoes
- Kartoffelpuffer (Potato Pancakes) with Applesauce
- Maultaschen Soup with Bread
- Käsespätzle with Roasted Onions and Salad
- Senfbraten (Mustard Roast) with Red Cabbage and Potato Dumplings
- Wurstsalat with Pretzel and Radishes
- Leberwurstbrot (Liverwurst Sandwich) with Pickles
- Semmelknödel (Bread Dumplings) with Mushroom Sauce and Salad
- Sauerbraten with Potato Pancakes and Red Cabbage
- Wurstsalat with German Bread and Pickles
- Labskaus with Rollmops and Pickled Beetroot
- Erbseneintopf (Split Pea Soup) with Frankfurters
- Gulaschsuppe with Rye Bread
- Käsespätzle with Salad
- Himmel und Erde (Heaven and Earth) with Blood Sausage

Schnitzel with Potato Salad

Ingredients:

For the schnitzel:

- 4 pork or veal schnitzel (about 150g each)
- Salt and pepper to taste
- Flour for dredging
- 2 eggs, beaten
- Bread crumbs
- Vegetable oil for frying
- Lemon wedges for serving

For the potato salad:

- 1 kg potatoes, boiled and peeled
- 1 red onion, finely chopped
- 4-5 pickles, finely chopped
- 2 tablespoons pickle juice
- 4 tablespoons mayonnaise
- 2 tablespoons mustard
- Salt and pepper to taste
- Chopped fresh parsley for garnish (optional)

Instructions:

1. Pound the schnitzel with a meat mallet until they are about 1/4 inch thick. Season them with salt and pepper.
2. Set up a breading station with three shallow bowls: one with flour, one with beaten eggs, and one with bread crumbs.
3. Dredge each schnitzel in the flour, then dip it in the beaten eggs, and finally coat it with bread crumbs, pressing gently to adhere.
4. Heat vegetable oil in a large skillet over medium-high heat. Fry the schnitzel for 3-4 minutes on each side, or until golden brown and cooked through. Drain on paper towels.
5. For the potato salad, cut the boiled potatoes into bite-sized pieces and place them in a large bowl.

6. Add the chopped red onion and pickles to the bowl with the potatoes.
7. In a small bowl, whisk together the pickle juice, mayonnaise, and mustard until well combined. Pour the dressing over the potato mixture and toss until evenly coated. Season with salt and pepper to taste.
8. Serve the schnitzel hot with the potato salad on the side. Garnish with chopped fresh parsley and lemon wedges.

Enjoy your classic Schnitzel with Potato Salad!

Beef Rouladen with Red Cabbage and Spaetzle

Ingredients:

For the Rouladen:

- 4 beef rouladen (thinly sliced beef)
- 4 slices bacon
- 1 large onion, finely chopped
- 2 dill pickles, sliced lengthwise
- 2 tablespoons mustard
- Salt and pepper to taste
- 2 tablespoons vegetable oil
- 2 cups beef broth
- 1/2 cup red wine (optional)
- 2 tablespoons all-purpose flour
- Chopped fresh parsley for garnish (optional)

For the Red Cabbage:

- 1 small red cabbage, thinly sliced
- 2 tablespoons butter
- 1 onion, thinly sliced
- 2 tablespoons red wine vinegar
- 2 tablespoons sugar
- Salt and pepper to taste

For the Spaetzle:

- 2 cups all-purpose flour
- 4 large eggs
- 1/2 cup milk
- Salt and pepper to taste
- Butter for frying

Instructions:

1. Preheat your oven to 350°F (175°C).
2. Lay the beef rouladen flat on a work surface. Place a slice of bacon, some chopped onion, and a pickle slice on each rouladen. Spread mustard over the filling. Season with salt and pepper.
3. Roll up each rouladen and secure with toothpicks or kitchen twine.
4. Heat vegetable oil in a large skillet over medium-high heat. Brown the rouladen on all sides, about 3-4 minutes per side.
5. Transfer the browned rouladen to a baking dish. Pour beef broth and red wine (if using) over the rouladen.
6. Cover the baking dish with foil and bake in the preheated oven for about 1.5 to 2 hours, or until the meat is tender.
7. While the rouladen are baking, prepare the red cabbage. In a large skillet, melt butter over medium heat. Add sliced onion and cook until softened. Add sliced red cabbage, red wine vinegar, sugar, salt, and pepper. Cook, stirring occasionally, until the cabbage is tender, about 20-30 minutes.
8. For the spaetzle, in a large bowl, whisk together flour, eggs, milk, salt, and pepper until smooth. The batter should be thick but pourable.
9. Bring a large pot of salted water to a boil. Using a spaetzle maker or a colander with large holes, press the batter through into the boiling water. Cook the spaetzle for 2-3 minutes, or until they float to the surface. Remove with a slotted spoon and transfer to a bowl.
10. In a large skillet, melt butter over medium heat. Add the cooked spaetzle and sauté until lightly browned.
11. Once the rouladen are cooked, remove them from the oven and transfer to a serving platter. Remove toothpicks or kitchen twine.
12. In a small bowl, mix together flour and water to make a slurry. Stir the slurry into the pan juices to thicken the sauce.
13. Serve the beef rouladen with the red cabbage and spaetzle. Garnish with chopped fresh parsley if desired.

Enjoy your Beef Rouladen with Red Cabbage and Spaetzle!

Goulash with Bread Dumplings

Ingredients:

For the Goulash:

- 2 lbs beef stew meat, cut into bite-sized pieces
- 2 tablespoons vegetable oil
- 2 onions, chopped
- 2 cloves garlic, minced
- 2 tablespoons sweet paprika
- 1 teaspoon caraway seeds
- 1 tablespoon tomato paste
- 2 cups beef broth
- 1 cup crushed tomatoes
- Salt and pepper to taste
- Chopped fresh parsley for garnish (optional)

For the Bread Dumplings:

- 4 slices stale bread, cubed
- 1/2 cup milk
- 2 eggs
- 2 tablespoons chopped fresh parsley
- Salt and pepper to taste
- 2 tablespoons all-purpose flour

Instructions:

1. In a large Dutch oven or heavy-bottomed pot, heat the vegetable oil over medium-high heat. Add the chopped onions and cook until softened, about 5 minutes.
2. Add the minced garlic, sweet paprika, and caraway seeds to the pot. Cook for another minute until fragrant.
3. Add the beef stew meat to the pot and brown on all sides, about 5-7 minutes.
4. Stir in the tomato paste until well combined with the meat and onion mixture.

5. Pour in the beef broth and crushed tomatoes, stirring to combine. Season with salt and pepper to taste.
6. Bring the mixture to a boil, then reduce the heat to low. Cover and simmer for 1.5 to 2 hours, or until the beef is tender and the sauce has thickened.
7. While the goulash is simmering, prepare the bread dumplings. In a bowl, soak the cubed stale bread in milk until softened.
8. Once the bread has soaked up the milk, add the eggs, chopped parsley, salt, pepper, and flour to the bowl. Mix until well combined.
9. Form the mixture into small dumplings, about the size of golf balls.
10. Bring a large pot of salted water to a boil. Carefully drop the dumplings into the boiling water and cook for about 15-20 minutes, or until they are cooked through and float to the surface.
11. Remove the cooked dumplings from the water with a slotted spoon and drain on paper towels.
12. Serve the goulash hot, garnished with chopped fresh parsley if desired, and accompanied by the bread dumplings.

Enjoy your hearty and flavorful Goulash with Bread Dumplings!

Currywurst with Fries

Ingredients:

For the Currywurst:

- 4 bratwurst sausages
- 1 cup ketchup
- 2 tablespoons curry powder
- 1 tablespoon Worcestershire sauce
- 1 tablespoon brown sugar
- Salt and pepper to taste
- Vegetable oil for frying

For the Fries:

- 4 large potatoes, peeled and cut into fries
- Vegetable oil for frying
- Salt to taste

Instructions:

1. Start by preparing the Currywurst sauce. In a small saucepan, combine the ketchup, curry powder, Worcestershire sauce, brown sugar, salt, and pepper. Stir well to combine. Bring the sauce to a simmer over medium heat and let it cook for about 5 minutes, stirring occasionally. Remove from heat and set aside.
2. Heat vegetable oil in a large skillet over medium-high heat. Add the bratwurst sausages and cook until browned and cooked through, about 8-10 minutes, turning occasionally.
3. While the sausages are cooking, prepare the fries. Heat vegetable oil in a deep fryer or large pot to 350°F (175°C). Carefully add the potato fries in batches and fry until golden brown and crispy, about 5-7 minutes per batch. Remove from the oil using a slotted spoon and drain on paper towels. Season with salt while still hot.
4. Once the sausages are cooked, remove them from the skillet and slice them into bite-sized pieces. Place them on a serving platter.

5. Pour the warm Currywurst sauce over the sliced sausages, coating them evenly.
6. Serve the Currywurst with the crispy fries on the side.
7. Optionally, you can sprinkle additional curry powder over the top of the Currywurst for extra flavor.

Enjoy your delicious Currywurst with Fries, a classic German street food dish!

Jägerschnitzel with Mushroom Gravy and Mashed Potatoes

Ingredients:

For the Jägerschnitzel:

- 4 pork schnitzel or veal cutlets, pounded thin
- Salt and pepper to taste
- 1/2 cup all-purpose flour
- 2 eggs, beaten
- 1 cup bread crumbs
- 2 tablespoons vegetable oil
- 2 tablespoons butter

For the Mushroom Gravy:

- 2 tablespoons butter
- 1 onion, finely chopped
- 2 cloves garlic, minced
- 8 oz mushrooms, sliced
- 2 tablespoons all-purpose flour
- 1 cup beef broth
- 1/2 cup heavy cream
- Salt and pepper to taste
- Chopped fresh parsley for garnish (optional)

For the Mashed Potatoes:

- 2 lbs potatoes, peeled and cut into chunks
- 4 tablespoons butter
- 1/2 cup milk
- Salt and pepper to taste

Instructions:

1. Start by preparing the mashed potatoes. Place the potato chunks in a large pot and cover with cold water. Bring to a boil and cook until the potatoes are tender, about 15-20 minutes. Drain the potatoes and return them to the pot.
2. Add butter, milk, salt, and pepper to the pot with the potatoes. Mash until smooth and creamy. Keep warm until ready to serve.
3. Season the pork schnitzel or veal cutlets with salt and pepper.
4. Set up a breading station with three shallow bowls: one with flour, one with beaten eggs, and one with bread crumbs.
5. Dredge each schnitzel in the flour, then dip it in the beaten eggs, and finally coat it with bread crumbs, pressing gently to adhere.
6. Heat vegetable oil and butter in a large skillet over medium-high heat. Add the breaded schnitzel to the skillet and cook until golden brown and cooked through, about 3-4 minutes per side. Remove from the skillet and keep warm.
7. In the same skillet, melt butter over medium heat. Add the chopped onion and garlic, and cook until softened, about 2-3 minutes. Add the sliced mushrooms and cook until they release their moisture and become golden brown, about 5-7 minutes.
8. Sprinkle the flour over the mushrooms and cook for 1-2 minutes, stirring constantly.
9. Gradually add the beef broth and heavy cream to the skillet, stirring constantly to prevent lumps from forming. Cook until the gravy thickens, about 5 minutes. Season with salt and pepper to taste.
10. To serve, spoon the mushroom gravy over the cooked schnitzel. Garnish with chopped fresh parsley if desired. Serve with mashed potatoes on the side.

Enjoy your delicious Jägerschnitzel with Mushroom Gravy and Mashed Potatoes!

Lentil Soup with Frankfurters

Ingredients:

- 1 cup green or brown lentils, rinsed and drained
- 1 onion, chopped
- 2 carrots, chopped
- 2 celery stalks, chopped
- 2 cloves garlic, minced
- 1 bay leaf
- 1 teaspoon dried thyme
- 1 teaspoon dried oregano
- 1 teaspoon paprika
- 6 cups chicken or vegetable broth
- Salt and pepper to taste
- 4 Frankfurter sausages, sliced
- Chopped fresh parsley for garnish (optional)

Instructions:

1. In a large pot or Dutch oven, heat a bit of oil over medium heat. Add the chopped onion, carrots, and celery. Cook until the vegetables are softened, about 5-7 minutes.
2. Add the minced garlic, bay leaf, dried thyme, dried oregano, and paprika to the pot. Cook for another minute until fragrant.
3. Add the rinsed lentils and chicken or vegetable broth to the pot. Bring the mixture to a boil, then reduce the heat to low. Cover and simmer for about 20-25 minutes, or until the lentils are tender.
4. Once the lentils are tender, use an immersion blender to blend the soup until smooth. Alternatively, you can blend a portion of the soup in a blender until smooth and return it to the pot.
5. Add the sliced Frankfurter sausages to the pot and simmer for another 5-7 minutes, or until the sausages are heated through.
6. Season the soup with salt and pepper to taste.
7. Ladle the Lentil Soup with Frankfurters into bowls and garnish with chopped fresh parsley if desired.
8. Serve the soup hot with crusty bread or rolls on the side.

Enjoy your comforting Lentil Soup with Frankfurters!

Königsberger Klopse (Meatballs in Caper Sauce) with Boiled Potatoes

Ingredients:

For the Meatballs:

- 1 lb ground beef
- 1 lb ground pork
- 1 onion, finely chopped
- 2 slices of bread, soaked in water and squeezed dry
- 2 eggs
- 2 tablespoons chopped fresh parsley
- Salt and pepper to taste
- All-purpose flour for dusting
- Vegetable oil for frying

For the Caper Sauce:

- 2 tablespoons butter
- 2 tablespoons all-purpose flour
- 2 cups beef broth
- 1/2 cup heavy cream
- 2 tablespoons capers, drained
- 2 tablespoons lemon juice
- Salt and pepper to taste

For serving:

- Boiled potatoes

Instructions:

1. In a large bowl, combine the ground beef, ground pork, finely chopped onion, soaked and squeezed bread, eggs, chopped parsley, salt, and pepper. Mix until well combined.
2. Shape the meat mixture into small meatballs, about the size of golf balls. Roll each meatball in flour to coat lightly.
3. Heat vegetable oil in a large skillet over medium-high heat. Add the meatballs in batches and fry until browned on all sides, about 5-7 minutes. Remove the meatballs from the skillet and set aside.
4. In the same skillet, melt butter over medium heat. Add flour and cook, stirring constantly, for 1-2 minutes to make a roux.
5. Gradually add beef broth to the skillet, stirring constantly to prevent lumps from forming. Cook until the sauce thickens, about 3-5 minutes.
6. Stir in heavy cream, capers, and lemon juice. Season with salt and pepper to taste.
7. Return the meatballs to the skillet and simmer in the sauce for another 10-15 minutes, or until the meatballs are cooked through and the sauce is heated through.
8. Serve the Königsberger Klopse with boiled potatoes on the side.

Enjoy your flavorful Königsberger Klopse with Meatballs in Caper Sauce and boiled potatoes!

Sauerbraten with Potato Dumplings and Red Cabbage

Ingredients:

For the Sauerbraten:

- 3-4 lbs beef roast (such as bottom round or rump roast)
- 1 onion, sliced
- 2 carrots, sliced
- 2 celery stalks, sliced
- 4 cloves garlic, minced
- 1 cup red wine vinegar
- 1 cup water
- 1 cup beef broth
- 1/4 cup brown sugar
- 1 tablespoon whole cloves
- 1 tablespoon whole peppercorns
- 2 bay leaves
- 2 tablespoons vegetable oil
- Salt and pepper to taste

For the Potato Dumplings:

- 4 large potatoes, peeled and quartered
- 1 cup all-purpose flour
- 2 eggs
- 1/4 cup breadcrumbs
- Salt and pepper to taste

For the Red Cabbage:

- 1 small head red cabbage, thinly sliced
- 1 onion, thinly sliced
- 2 apples, peeled, cored, and sliced
- 1/4 cup red wine vinegar
- 1/4 cup apple cider vinegar

- 1/4 cup brown sugar
- 1/2 cup water
- Salt and pepper to taste

Instructions:

1. In a large bowl, combine the sliced onion, carrots, celery, minced garlic, red wine vinegar, water, beef broth, brown sugar, whole cloves, whole peppercorns, and bay leaves. Place the beef roast in the marinade, making sure it's fully submerged. Cover and refrigerate for 3-5 days, turning the roast occasionally.
2. After marinating, remove the beef roast from the marinade and pat dry with paper towels. Strain the marinade and reserve the liquid and vegetables separately.
3. Preheat the oven to 325°F (160°C).
4. Heat vegetable oil in a Dutch oven or large oven-safe pot over medium-high heat. Brown the beef roast on all sides, about 5-7 minutes per side. Remove the roast and set aside.
5. In the same pot, add the strained vegetables from the marinade and cook until softened, about 5 minutes.
6. Return the beef roast to the pot and pour in the reserved marinade liquid. Cover the pot and transfer it to the preheated oven. Roast for 3-4 hours, or until the beef is tender and can be easily pierced with a fork.
7. While the beef is roasting, prepare the potato dumplings. Cook the quartered potatoes in boiling salted water until tender, about 15-20 minutes. Drain the potatoes and mash them while they're still warm.
8. In a large bowl, combine the mashed potatoes, flour, eggs, breadcrumbs, salt, and pepper. Mix until well combined. Shape the mixture into dumplings about the size of golf balls.
9. Bring a large pot of salted water to a boil. Carefully drop the dumplings into the boiling water and cook for about 15-20 minutes, or until they float to the surface. Remove with a slotted spoon and drain on paper towels.
10. For the red cabbage, combine the sliced red cabbage, sliced onion, sliced apples, red wine vinegar, apple cider vinegar, brown sugar, water, salt, and pepper in a large pot. Bring to a boil, then reduce the heat to low and simmer, covered, for about 45-60 minutes, or until the cabbage is tender.
11. Once the beef roast is done, remove it from the pot and let it rest for a few minutes before slicing.
12. Serve the Sauerbraten slices with the potato dumplings and red cabbage. Spoon some of the cooking liquid over the beef slices as a sauce.

Enjoy your delicious Sauerbraten with Potato Dumplings and Red Cabbage, a comforting and satisfying German meal!

Kasseler Ripchen with Sauerkraut and Mash

Ingredients:

For the Kasseler Ripchen:

- 4 Kasseler pork chops
- Salt and pepper to taste
- 2 tablespoons vegetable oil

For the Sauerkraut:

- 1 lb sauerkraut, drained and rinsed
- 1 onion, chopped
- 2 cloves garlic, minced
- 2 tablespoons vegetable oil
- 1 tablespoon caraway seeds
- 1 tablespoon brown sugar
- Salt and pepper to taste

For the Mash:

- 2 lbs potatoes, peeled and cut into chunks
- 4 tablespoons butter
- 1/2 cup milk
- Salt and pepper to taste

Instructions:

1. Preheat your oven to 375°F (190°C).
2. Season the Kasseler pork chops with salt and pepper on both sides.
3. Heat vegetable oil in a large skillet over medium-high heat. Add the pork chops to the skillet and sear on both sides until golden brown, about 3-4 minutes per side.
4. Transfer the seared pork chops to a baking dish and bake in the preheated oven for 20-25 minutes, or until cooked through.

5. While the pork chops are baking, prepare the sauerkraut. Heat vegetable oil in a large pot over medium heat. Add the chopped onion and minced garlic to the pot and cook until softened, about 5 minutes.
6. Add the drained and rinsed sauerkraut to the pot, along with the caraway seeds and brown sugar. Stir well to combine. Season with salt and pepper to taste. Cover and simmer for about 15-20 minutes, stirring occasionally.
7. While the sauerkraut is simmering, prepare the mashed potatoes. Place the potato chunks in a large pot and cover with cold water. Bring to a boil and cook until the potatoes are tender, about 15-20 minutes. Drain the potatoes and return them to the pot.
8. Add butter, milk, salt, and pepper to the pot with the potatoes. Mash until smooth and creamy. Keep warm until ready to serve.
9. Once the pork chops are done baking, remove them from the oven and let them rest for a few minutes before serving.
10. Serve the Kasseler Ripchen hot with sauerkraut and mashed potatoes on the side.

Enjoy your hearty and flavorful Kasseler Ripchen with Sauerkraut and Mash!

Leberkäse with Fried Eggs and Potato Salad

Ingredients:

For the Leberkäse:

- 1 lb ground pork
- 1 lb ground beef
- 1 onion, finely chopped
- 2 cloves garlic, minced
- 1/2 cup breadcrumbs
- 1/4 cup milk
- 2 eggs
- 1 tablespoon mustard
- 1 teaspoon salt
- 1/2 teaspoon black pepper
- 1/2 teaspoon ground marjoram
- 1/2 teaspoon ground paprika

For the Fried Eggs:

- 4 eggs
- Salt and pepper to taste
- Butter or oil for frying

For the Potato Salad:

- 2 lbs potatoes, peeled and cut into cubes
- 1/2 cup mayonnaise
- 2 tablespoons mustard
- 1 onion, finely chopped
- 2 dill pickles, finely chopped
- Salt and pepper to taste
- Chopped fresh parsley for garnish (optional)

Instructions:

1. Preheat your oven to 350°F (175°C).
2. In a large mixing bowl, combine the ground pork, ground beef, finely chopped onion, minced garlic, breadcrumbs, milk, eggs, mustard, salt, pepper, marjoram, and paprika. Mix until well combined.
3. Transfer the mixture to a greased loaf pan and smooth the top.
4. Bake the Leberkäse in the preheated oven for 60-70 minutes, or until cooked through and golden brown on top. Remove from the oven and let it cool for a few minutes before slicing.
5. While the Leberkäse is baking, prepare the potato salad. Boil the cubed potatoes in salted water until tender, about 10-15 minutes. Drain and let cool slightly.
6. In a large bowl, combine the mayonnaise, mustard, chopped onion, chopped dill pickles, salt, and pepper. Add the cooked potatoes and toss until evenly coated. Adjust seasoning if necessary. Refrigerate until ready to serve.
7. In a skillet, heat butter or oil over medium heat. Crack the eggs into the skillet and fry until the whites are set and the yolks are still runny. Season with salt and pepper.
8. To serve, slice the Leberkäse and serve with fried eggs and potato salad on the side. Garnish the potato salad with chopped fresh parsley if desired.

Enjoy your delicious Leberkäse with Fried Eggs and Potato Salad!

Maultaschen (Swabian Ravioli) with Salad

Ingredients:

For the Maultaschen dough:

- 2 cups all-purpose flour
- 2 eggs
- 1/4 cup water
- 1/2 teaspoon salt

For the filling:

- 1 lb ground meat (pork, beef, or a combination)
- 1 onion, finely chopped
- 2 cloves garlic, minced
- 2 cups fresh spinach, chopped
- 1/2 cup breadcrumbs
- 2 eggs
- 1/4 cup milk
- 1 teaspoon salt
- 1/2 teaspoon black pepper
- 1/2 teaspoon nutmeg
- 1/2 teaspoon paprika
- 1/4 teaspoon ground cloves

For the salad:

- Mixed greens (lettuce, arugula, spinach, etc.)
- Cherry tomatoes, halved
- Cucumber, sliced
- Red onion, thinly sliced
- Salad dressing of your choice

Instructions:

1. Start by making the Maultaschen dough. In a large mixing bowl, combine the flour and salt. Make a well in the center and add the eggs and water. Mix until a dough forms, then knead on a floured surface for about 5 minutes until smooth. Wrap the dough in plastic wrap and let it rest for at least 30 minutes.
2. While the dough is resting, prepare the filling. In a skillet, cook the ground meat over medium heat until browned. Add the chopped onion and garlic, and cook until softened. Stir in the chopped spinach and cook until wilted. Remove from heat and let cool slightly.
3. In a separate bowl, mix together the breadcrumbs, eggs, milk, salt, pepper, nutmeg, paprika, and ground cloves. Add this mixture to the meat and spinach mixture, and stir until well combined.
4. Roll out the Maultaschen dough on a floured surface until it is about 1/8 inch thick. Cut the dough into squares, about 3-4 inches in size.
5. Place a spoonful of the filling in the center of each dough square. Fold the dough over the filling to form a triangle, then press the edges together firmly to seal.
6. Bring a large pot of salted water to a boil. Carefully drop the Maultaschen into the boiling water and cook for about 8-10 minutes, or until they float to the surface. Remove with a slotted spoon and drain.
7. While the Maultaschen are cooking, prepare the salad. In a large bowl, toss together the mixed greens, cherry tomatoes, cucumber slices, and thinly sliced red onion. Drizzle with your favorite salad dressing and toss to coat.
8. Serve the cooked Maultaschen hot alongside the salad.

Enjoy your delicious Maultaschen with Salad, a comforting and satisfying German meal!

Labskaus (Corned Beef Hash) with Fried Egg and Pickles

Ingredients:

For the Labskaus:

- 1 lb corned beef, finely chopped
- 4 large potatoes, peeled and diced
- 1 onion, finely chopped
- 2-3 cooked beets, finely chopped (optional)
- 2 tablespoons butter or oil
- Salt and pepper to taste
- 4 eggs
- Pickles, for serving

Instructions:

1. In a large skillet, heat the butter or oil over medium heat. Add the chopped onions and sauté until softened and translucent, about 5 minutes.
2. Add the finely chopped corned beef to the skillet and cook until heated through, stirring occasionally, for about 5-7 minutes.
3. Add the diced potatoes to the skillet and cook until tender, about 10-15 minutes, stirring occasionally. If using cooked beets, add them to the skillet and cook until heated through.
4. Season the Labskaus mixture with salt and pepper to taste. Adjust seasoning if necessary.
5. While the Labskaus is cooking, fry the eggs in a separate skillet to your desired doneness.
6. To serve, divide the Labskaus mixture among plates. Top each serving with a fried egg and serve with pickles on the side.
7. Enjoy your Labskaus with Fried Egg and Pickles, a comforting and hearty German meal!

Grünkohl (Kale) with Pinkel Sausage and Boiled Potatoes

Ingredients:

For the Grünkohl:

- 2 lbs kale, stems removed and leaves chopped
- 1 onion, finely chopped
- 2 cloves garlic, minced
- 4 slices bacon, chopped
- 1 Pinkel sausage (or substitute with another smoked sausage)
- 2 tablespoons vegetable oil
- 2 cups beef or vegetable broth
- 1 teaspoon caraway seeds
- Salt and pepper to taste

For the Boiled Potatoes:

- 1 lb potatoes, peeled and quartered
- Salt for boiling

Instructions:

1. In a large pot, heat the vegetable oil over medium heat. Add the chopped onion, minced garlic, and chopped bacon. Cook until the onion is softened and the bacon is crispy, about 5-7 minutes.
2. Add the chopped kale to the pot, along with the caraway seeds. Stir well to combine.
3. Pour the beef or vegetable broth into the pot. Bring to a boil, then reduce the heat to low. Cover and simmer for about 45-60 minutes, or until the kale is tender, stirring occasionally.
4. While the kale is cooking, prepare the Pinkel sausage. If it's raw, cook it according to the package instructions. If it's pre-cooked, you can slice it and add it to the kale during the last 10-15 minutes of cooking to heat through.
5. About 20 minutes before the kale is done cooking, prepare the boiled potatoes. Place the peeled and quartered potatoes in a large pot and cover with cold water.

Add a pinch of salt to the water. Bring to a boil, then reduce the heat to medium-low and simmer for about 15-20 minutes, or until the potatoes are fork-tender.
6. Once the kale is tender and the Pinkel sausage is heated through, season the Grünkohl with salt and pepper to taste.
7. Drain the boiled potatoes and serve them alongside the Grünkohl and Pinkel sausage.
8. Enjoy your hearty Grünkohl with Pinkel Sausage and Boiled Potatoes, a comforting and traditional German meal!

Bratwurst with Sauerkraut and Mustard

Ingredients:

- Bratwurst sausages
- Sauerkraut, drained
- Mustard (your favorite variety)
- Vegetable oil or butter (optional)

Instructions:

1. Preheat your grill or grill pan to medium-high heat.
2. If using raw bratwurst sausages, you can cook them directly on the grill. Brush them with a little vegetable oil or butter to prevent sticking if desired. Grill the sausages for about 10-12 minutes, turning occasionally, until they are cooked through and have nice grill marks.
3. If using pre-cooked bratwurst sausages, you can heat them on the grill for about 5-7 minutes, turning occasionally, until they are heated through and have grill marks.
4. While the bratwurst is cooking, heat the sauerkraut in a separate skillet over medium heat. You can add a little vegetable oil or butter to the skillet if desired. Cook the sauerkraut for about 5-7 minutes, stirring occasionally, until it is heated through.
5. Once the bratwurst sausages are cooked and the sauerkraut is heated, serve them together on plates. Serve the mustard on the side for dipping or drizzle it over the sausages and sauerkraut.
6. Enjoy your delicious Bratwurst with Sauerkraut and Mustard, a classic German dish that's perfect for any occasion!

Beef Rouladen with Potato Dumplings and Green Beans

Ingredients:

For the beef rouladen:

- 4 beef rouladen (thinly sliced beef)
- 4 slices bacon
- 1 onion, finely chopped
- 4 dill pickles, sliced lengthwise
- 2 tablespoons mustard
- Salt and pepper to taste
- Toothpicks or kitchen twine for securing

For the potato dumplings:

- 4 large potatoes, peeled and quartered
- 1 egg
- 1/2 cup all-purpose flour
- Salt to taste
- Water for boiling

For the green beans:

- 1 lb fresh green beans, trimmed
- Salt to taste
- Butter for sautéing (optional)

Instructions:

1. Preheat your oven to 350°F (175°C).
2. Lay out the beef rouladen slices on a flat surface. Spread each slice with mustard. Place a slice of bacon, some chopped onion, and a pickle slice on each rouladen. Roll up the rouladen and secure with toothpicks or kitchen twine.

3. Heat some oil in a large skillet over medium-high heat. Brown the rouladen on all sides, about 2-3 minutes per side. Remove from the skillet and place in a baking dish.
4. Cover the baking dish with foil and bake the rouladen in the preheated oven for about 1.5 to 2 hours, or until the beef is tender.
5. While the rouladen is baking, prepare the potato dumplings. Cook the peeled and quartered potatoes in boiling salted water until tender, about 15-20 minutes. Drain the potatoes and let them cool slightly.
6. Mash the cooked potatoes or pass them through a ricer. Let cool slightly. Add the egg, flour, and salt to the mashed potatoes and mix until a dough forms.
7. Divide the dough into 4 equal portions and shape each portion into a dumpling. Bring a large pot of salted water to a boil. Carefully drop the dumplings into the boiling water and cook for about 15-20 minutes, or until they float to the surface.
8. While the dumplings are cooking, prepare the green beans. Bring a pot of salted water to a boil. Add the trimmed green beans and cook for about 5-7 minutes, or until tender-crisp. Drain the green beans and toss with butter if desired.
9. Once everything is cooked, remove the rouladen from the oven and let them rest for a few minutes before serving.
10. Serve the beef rouladen with potato dumplings and green beans on the side. Enjoy your delicious and comforting German meal!

Senfeier (Mustard Eggs) with Potatoes

Ingredients:

For the Senfeier:

- 6 hard-boiled eggs, peeled and halved
- 2 tablespoons butter
- 2 tablespoons all-purpose flour
- 1 cup milk
- 3 tablespoons mustard (preferably German mustard)
- Salt and pepper to taste
- Chopped fresh parsley for garnish (optional)

For the Potatoes:

- 4 large potatoes, peeled and quartered
- Salt for boiling

Instructions:

1. Start by preparing the hard-boiled eggs. Place the eggs in a saucepan and cover them with cold water. Bring the water to a boil over high heat, then reduce the heat to medium-low and let the eggs simmer for about 10-12 minutes. Remove the eggs from the heat, drain the hot water, and transfer the eggs to a bowl of ice water to cool. Once cooled, peel the eggs and cut them in half lengthwise.
2. While the eggs are cooking, prepare the potatoes. Place the peeled and quartered potatoes in a large pot and cover them with cold water. Add a pinch of salt to the water. Bring to a boil, then reduce the heat to medium-low and let the potatoes simmer for about 15-20 minutes, or until they are fork-tender.
3. In a saucepan, melt the butter over medium heat. Add the flour and cook, stirring constantly, for about 1-2 minutes to make a roux.
4. Gradually whisk in the milk, stirring constantly to prevent lumps from forming. Cook until the sauce thickens, about 3-5 minutes.
5. Stir in the mustard, salt, and pepper to taste. Adjust seasoning if necessary.
6. Carefully add the halved hard-boiled eggs to the mustard sauce, making sure they are coated evenly. Let the eggs simmer in the sauce for another 2-3 minutes to heat through.

7. Drain the boiled potatoes and serve them alongside the Senfeier.
8. Garnish the Senfeier with chopped fresh parsley if desired.
9. Serve the Senfeier with Potatoes hot, and enjoy your delicious and comforting German meal!

Labskaus with Rollmops and Pickled Onions

Ingredients:

For the Labskaus:

- 1 lb corned beef or salted meat
- 4 large potatoes, peeled and diced
- 2 onions, finely chopped
- 2 large beets, cooked and finely chopped (optional)
- 4 rollmops (pickled herring fillets)
- Pickled onions, for serving
- 2 tablespoons butter or vegetable oil
- Salt and pepper to taste

Instructions:

1. In a large pot, cover the corned beef or salted meat with water and bring to a boil. Reduce the heat and simmer for about 1.5 to 2 hours, or until the meat is tender. Remove the meat from the pot and let it cool slightly. Reserve the cooking liquid.
2. In another pot, boil the diced potatoes in salted water until tender, about 15-20 minutes. Drain and set aside.
3. In a skillet, melt the butter or heat the vegetable oil over medium heat. Add the chopped onions and cook until soft and translucent, about 5-7 minutes.
4. While the onions are cooking, finely chop the cooked corned beef or salted meat. Add it to the skillet with the onions and cook for another 5 minutes, stirring occasionally.
5. Add the cooked potatoes to the skillet with the meat and onions. If using cooked beets, add them now as well. Mash everything together with a potato masher until well combined. If the mixture is too dry, you can add some of the reserved cooking liquid from the meat to moisten it.
6. Season the Labskaus with salt and pepper to taste.
7. To serve, divide the Labskaus among plates. Top each portion with a rollmop and serve with pickled onions on the side.
8. Enjoy your Labskaus with rollmops and pickled onions, a classic and hearty German dish!

Flammkuchen (German Pizza) with Salad

Ingredients:

For the Flammkuchen:

- 1 pre-made pizza dough or Flammkuchen dough
- 1/2 cup sour cream or crème fraîche
- 1 onion, thinly sliced
- 4 slices bacon, chopped
- Salt and pepper to taste
- Fresh chives or parsley, chopped (optional, for garnish)

For the Salad:

- Mixed greens (lettuce, arugula, spinach, etc.)
- Cherry tomatoes, halved
- Cucumber, sliced
- Red onion, thinly sliced
- Salad dressing of your choice

Instructions:

1. Preheat your oven to the highest temperature possible, ideally with a pizza stone inside if you have one.
2. Roll out the pizza dough or Flammkuchen dough on a lightly floured surface until very thin. Transfer the rolled-out dough to a baking sheet lined with parchment paper.
3. Spread the sour cream or crème fraîche evenly over the surface of the dough, leaving a small border around the edges.
4. Scatter the thinly sliced onions and chopped bacon over the sour cream or crème fraîche. Season with salt and pepper to taste.
5. Place the Flammkuchen in the preheated oven and bake for 10-12 minutes, or until the crust is crispy and the toppings are golden brown and bubbly.

6. While the Flammkuchen is baking, prepare the salad. In a large bowl, toss together the mixed greens, cherry tomatoes, sliced cucumber, and thinly sliced red onion. Drizzle with your favorite salad dressing and toss to coat.
7. Once the Flammkuchen is done baking, remove it from the oven and let it cool slightly. Sprinkle with chopped fresh chives or parsley if desired.
8. Serve the Flammkuchen hot, alongside the salad.
9. Enjoy your delicious Flammkuchen with Salad, a perfect combination of flavors for a satisfying meal!

Wurstsalat (Sausage Salad) with Bread

Ingredients:

For the Wurstsalat:

- 8 oz German sausages (such as Fleischwurst or Lyoner), thinly sliced
- 1 small onion, thinly sliced
- 2 small pickles, thinly sliced
- 2 tablespoons white wine vinegar
- 1 tablespoon olive oil
- 1 teaspoon mustard
- 1 teaspoon honey or sugar
- Salt and pepper to taste
- Chopped fresh parsley for garnish (optional)

For serving:

- Sliced bread or bread rolls

Instructions:

1. In a large bowl, combine the thinly sliced sausages, onion, and pickles.
2. In a small bowl, whisk together the white wine vinegar, olive oil, mustard, honey or sugar, salt, and pepper to make the vinaigrette.
3. Pour the vinaigrette over the sausage mixture and toss until everything is well coated. Let the salad marinate in the refrigerator for at least 30 minutes to allow the flavors to meld together.
4. Just before serving, sprinkle the Wurstsalat with chopped fresh parsley if desired.
5. Serve the Wurstsalat with sliced bread or bread rolls on the side.
6. Enjoy your delicious Wurstsalat with Bread, a classic German dish that's perfect for any occasion!

Käsespätzle (Cheese Spaetzle) with Fried Onions

Ingredients:

For the Spätzle:

- 2 cups all-purpose flour
- 4 eggs
- 1/2 cup milk
- 1/2 teaspoon salt
- 1/4 teaspoon nutmeg (optional)
- Water, as needed

For the Cheese Sauce:

- 2 cups grated Emmental cheese (or any Swiss cheese)
- 1/2 cup grated Gruyère cheese (optional, for extra flavor)
- 1/2 cup milk
- Salt and pepper to taste

For the Fried Onions:

- 2 large onions, thinly sliced
- 2 tablespoons all-purpose flour
- Vegetable oil for frying
- Salt to taste

Instructions:

1. Start by making the Spätzle dough. In a large mixing bowl, combine the flour, eggs, milk, salt, and nutmeg (if using). Mix until a smooth, thick batter forms. If the batter is too thick, add a little water to thin it out.
2. Bring a large pot of salted water to a boil. Using a Spätzle maker or a colander with large holes, press the batter through the holes into the boiling water. Cook

the Spätzle for about 2-3 minutes, or until they float to the surface. Remove them with a slotted spoon and transfer to a colander to drain.
3. Preheat your oven to 350°F (175°C). Grease a baking dish and set aside.
4. In a saucepan, heat the milk for the cheese sauce over medium heat. Once hot, gradually add the grated Emmental and Gruyère cheese, stirring constantly until melted and smooth. Season with salt and pepper to taste. Remove from heat.
5. In a large skillet, heat vegetable oil over medium-high heat. Toss the thinly sliced onions with flour until evenly coated. Fry the onions in the hot oil until golden and crispy, stirring occasionally. Remove them from the skillet and drain on paper towels.
6. Layer half of the cooked Spätzle in the prepared baking dish. Pour half of the cheese sauce over the Spätzle. Repeat with the remaining Spätzle and cheese sauce.
7. Sprinkle the crispy fried onions over the top of the Käsespätzle.
8. Bake in the preheated oven for 20-25 minutes, or until bubbly and golden brown on top.
9. Serve the Käsespätzle hot, garnished with additional chopped fresh parsley if desired.

Enjoy your delicious Käsespätzle with Fried Onions, a comforting and indulgent German dish!

Sülze (Head Cheese) with Potato Salad and Pickles

Ingredients:

For the Sülze:

- 2 lbs pig's head or calf's head, cleaned and trimmed (you can ask your butcher to do this)
- 1 onion, peeled and quartered
- 2 carrots, peeled and chopped
- 2 stalks celery, chopped
- 2 bay leaves
- 6 peppercorns
- Salt to taste
- Gelatin or aspic mix according to package instructions

For the Potato Salad:

- 2 lbs potatoes, peeled and diced
- 1 onion, finely chopped
- 2 tablespoons vinegar
- 3 tablespoons vegetable oil
- Salt and pepper to taste
- Chopped fresh parsley for garnish (optional)

For Serving:

- Pickles

Instructions:

1. Place the cleaned and trimmed pig's or calf's head in a large pot. Add enough water to cover the head completely.

2. Add the quartered onion, chopped carrots, chopped celery, bay leaves, peppercorns, and salt to the pot.
3. Bring the water to a boil, then reduce the heat to low and let the head simmer gently for 3-4 hours, or until the meat is tender and falling off the bone.
4. Remove the head from the pot and let it cool slightly. Strain the cooking liquid and discard the vegetables and spices. Reserve the liquid.
5. Once the head is cool enough to handle, remove the meat from the bones and chop it into small pieces. Discard any skin, bones, or gristle.
6. Pack the chopped meat into a loaf pan or mold. Pour enough of the reserved cooking liquid over the meat to cover it completely.
7. Prepare the gelatin or aspic mix according to the package instructions. Pour it over the meat in the pan to cover completely. Refrigerate the Sülze for at least 4 hours, or until set.
8. While the Sülze is chilling, prepare the potato salad. Boil the diced potatoes in salted water until tender, about 10-15 minutes. Drain and let them cool slightly.
9. In a large bowl, combine the cooked potatoes, finely chopped onion, vinegar, vegetable oil, salt, and pepper. Toss until well combined.
10. Once the Sülze is set, remove it from the refrigerator and unmold it onto a serving platter. Slice it thinly.
11. Serve the sliced Sülze with potato salad, pickles, and garnish with chopped fresh parsley if desired.

Enjoy your Sülze with Potato Salad and Pickles, a classic German dish that's perfect for a cold buffet or picnic!

Linseneintopf (Lentil Stew) with Sausage

Ingredients:

- 1 cup dried green or brown lentils, rinsed and drained
- 6 cups vegetable or chicken broth
- 2 tablespoons olive oil
- 1 onion, chopped
- 2 carrots, chopped
- 2 celery stalks, chopped
- 2 cloves garlic, minced
- 8 oz smoked sausage or bratwurst, sliced
- 1 bay leaf
- 1 teaspoon dried thyme
- Salt and pepper to taste
- Chopped fresh parsley for garnish (optional)

Instructions:

1. In a large pot, heat the olive oil over medium heat. Add the chopped onion, carrots, and celery. Cook, stirring occasionally, until the vegetables are softened, about 5-7 minutes.
2. Add the minced garlic to the pot and cook for an additional 1-2 minutes, until fragrant.
3. Stir in the sliced sausage or bratwurst and cook until lightly browned, about 5 minutes.
4. Add the rinsed lentils, bay leaf, and dried thyme to the pot. Pour in the vegetable or chicken broth.
5. Bring the mixture to a boil, then reduce the heat to low. Cover the pot and let the stew simmer for about 25-30 minutes, or until the lentils are tender.
6. Once the lentils are cooked, season the stew with salt and pepper to taste. Adjust seasoning if necessary.
7. Remove the bay leaf from the pot.
8. Ladle the Linseneintopf into bowls and garnish with chopped fresh parsley if desired.
9. Serve hot and enjoy your comforting Linseneintopf with Sausage, a delicious German dish perfect for chilly days!

Frikadellen (German Meatballs) with Potato Salad

Ingredients:

For the Frikadellen:

- 1 lb ground beef or a mixture of beef and pork
- 1 small onion, finely chopped
- 1 clove garlic, minced
- 1 egg
- 1/4 cup breadcrumbs
- 2 tablespoons milk
- 1 tablespoon mustard
- 1 tablespoon chopped fresh parsley
- Salt and pepper to taste
- Vegetable oil for frying

For the Potato Salad:

- 2 lbs potatoes, peeled and diced
- 1 small onion, finely chopped
- 2 tablespoons white vinegar
- 3 tablespoons vegetable oil
- 1 tablespoon mustard
- Salt and pepper to taste
- Chopped fresh parsley for garnish (optional)

Instructions:

1. Start by making the Frikadellen mixture. In a large mixing bowl, combine the ground beef, chopped onion, minced garlic, egg, breadcrumbs, milk, mustard, chopped parsley, salt, and pepper. Mix until everything is well combined.
2. Shape the Frikadellen mixture into small meatballs, about 1-2 inches in diameter.
3. Heat vegetable oil in a large skillet over medium heat. Once the oil is hot, add the Frikadellen to the skillet in batches, being careful not to overcrowd the pan. Cook the meatballs for about 5-6 minutes on each side, or until they are browned and cooked through.

4. While the Frikadellen are cooking, prepare the potato salad. Boil the diced potatoes in salted water until tender, about 10-15 minutes. Drain and let them cool slightly.
5. In a large bowl, combine the cooked potatoes, finely chopped onion, white vinegar, vegetable oil, mustard, salt, and pepper. Toss until everything is well coated.
6. Once the Frikadellen are cooked, remove them from the skillet and drain on paper towels.
7. Serve the Frikadellen hot alongside the potato salad.
8. Garnish the potato salad with chopped fresh parsley if desired.
9. Enjoy your delicious Frikadellen with Potato Salad, a classic and comforting German meal!

Käsesuppe (Cheese Soup) with Pretzel Rolls

Ingredients:

For the Cheese Soup:

- 4 tablespoons butter
- 1 onion, finely chopped
- 2 carrots, peeled and diced
- 2 celery stalks, diced
- 2 cloves garlic, minced
- 1/4 cup all-purpose flour
- 4 cups chicken or vegetable broth
- 2 cups milk
- 2 cups shredded cheddar cheese
- 1 cup shredded Gruyère cheese
- Salt and pepper to taste
- Chopped fresh chives or parsley for garnish (optional)

For the Pretzel Rolls:

- 4 soft pretzel rolls
- 2 tablespoons butter, melted
- Coarse salt for sprinkling

Instructions:

For the Cheese Soup:

1. In a large pot, melt the butter over medium heat. Add the chopped onion, diced carrots, and diced celery. Cook, stirring occasionally, until the vegetables are softened, about 5-7 minutes.
2. Add the minced garlic to the pot and cook for an additional 1-2 minutes, until fragrant.
3. Sprinkle the flour over the vegetables and stir to coat. Cook for 1-2 minutes to remove the raw flour taste.
4. Gradually pour in the chicken or vegetable broth, stirring constantly to prevent lumps from forming. Add the milk and bring the mixture to a simmer.

5. Let the soup simmer for about 10-15 minutes, stirring occasionally, until it thickens slightly.
6. Reduce the heat to low and gradually stir in the shredded cheddar and Gruyère cheese until melted and smooth. Season with salt and pepper to taste.
7. Serve the Käsesuppe hot, garnished with chopped fresh chives or parsley if desired.

For the Pretzel Rolls:

1. Preheat your oven to 350°F (175°C).
2. Slice the soft pretzel rolls in half horizontally. Brush the cut sides with melted butter and sprinkle with coarse salt.
3. Place the pretzel rolls on a baking sheet, cut side up, and bake in the preheated oven for 5-7 minutes, or until they are warmed through and the edges are slightly crispy.
4. Serve the warm Pretzel Rolls alongside the Käsesuppe for dipping.
5. Enjoy your delicious Käsesuppe with Pretzel Rolls, a comforting and satisfying meal!

Schweinshaxe (Pork Knuckle) with Sauerkraut and Bread Dumplings

Ingredients:

For the Schweinshaxe:

- 2 pork knuckles (about 2-3 lbs each)
- Salt and pepper to taste
- 2 tablespoons vegetable oil
- 1 onion, sliced
- 2 cloves garlic, minced
- 1 tablespoon caraway seeds
- 2 cups chicken or vegetable broth
- 1 cup beer (optional)
- 2 bay leaves
- 1 tablespoon honey or brown sugar

For the Sauerkraut:

- 1 lb sauerkraut, drained and rinsed
- 2 tablespoons butter
- 1 onion, thinly sliced
- 1 apple, peeled, cored, and sliced
- 1/4 cup white wine (optional)
- Salt and pepper to taste

For the Bread Dumplings:

- 4 slices stale bread, cubed
- 1/2 cup milk
- 2 eggs
- 2 tablespoons chopped fresh parsley
- Salt and pepper to taste
- 2 tablespoons butter, melted

Instructions:

For the Schweinshaxe:

1. Preheat your oven to 350°F (175°C).
2. Score the skin of the pork knuckles in a crosshatch pattern. Season the knuckles generously with salt and pepper.
3. Heat the vegetable oil in a large ovenproof skillet or Dutch oven over medium-high heat. Add the pork knuckles and sear on all sides until golden brown, about 5-7 minutes per side.
4. Remove the pork knuckles from the skillet and set aside. Add the sliced onion, minced garlic, and caraway seeds to the skillet and cook until the onions are soft and translucent, about 5 minutes.
5. Return the pork knuckles to the skillet. Add the chicken or vegetable broth, beer (if using), bay leaves, and honey or brown sugar.
6. Cover the skillet or Dutch oven with a lid or aluminum foil and transfer it to the preheated oven. Bake for 2-3 hours, or until the pork knuckles are tender and the skin is crispy.

For the Sauerkraut:

1. In a large skillet, melt the butter over medium heat. Add the thinly sliced onion and cook until soft and translucent, about 5 minutes.
2. Add the drained and rinsed sauerkraut to the skillet, along with the sliced apple and white wine (if using). Season with salt and pepper to taste.
3. Cover the skillet and let the sauerkraut simmer for about 20-30 minutes, stirring occasionally, until the flavors are well combined and the sauerkraut is tender.

For the Bread Dumplings:

1. In a large bowl, soak the cubed stale bread in the milk for about 10 minutes, until softened.
2. Add the eggs, chopped fresh parsley, salt, and pepper to the bread mixture. Mix until well combined.
3. Shape the bread mixture into golf ball-sized dumplings.

4. Bring a large pot of salted water to a simmer. Carefully drop the dumplings into the simmering water and cook for about 15-20 minutes, or until they float to the surface.
5. Remove the dumplings from the water with a slotted spoon and drain on paper towels. Brush with melted butter before serving.

To serve:

1. Serve the Schweinshaxe hot, accompanied by the sauerkraut and bread dumplings.
2. Enjoy your hearty and delicious Schweinshaxe with Sauerkraut and Bread Dumplings, a classic German dish that's perfect for a comforting meal!

Käsespätzle with Caramelized Onions and Salad

Ingredients:

For the Käsespätzle:

- 1 batch of Spätzle dough (you can use store-bought or homemade)
- 2 tablespoons butter
- 2 onions, thinly sliced
- 2 cups grated Emmental cheese (or any Swiss cheese)
- Salt and pepper to taste
- Chopped fresh parsley for garnish (optional)

For the Salad:

- Mixed greens (lettuce, arugula, spinach, etc.)
- Cherry tomatoes, halved
- Cucumber, sliced
- Red onion, thinly sliced
- Salad dressing of your choice

Instructions:

1. Prepare the Spätzle dough according to your chosen recipe or package instructions. Once the dough is ready, bring a large pot of salted water to a boil.
2. Using a Spätzle maker, colander, or spoon, press the dough through the holes into the boiling water. Cook the Spätzle until they float to the surface, then remove them with a slotted spoon and transfer them to a colander to drain.
3. In a large skillet, melt the butter over medium heat. Add the thinly sliced onions and cook, stirring occasionally, until they are soft and caramelized, about 20-25 minutes.
4. Preheat your oven to 350°F (175°C). Grease a baking dish and set aside.
5. In a large mixing bowl, combine the cooked Spätzle with the grated Emmental cheese. Season with salt and pepper to taste.

6. Transfer half of the Spätzle mixture to the prepared baking dish. Top with half of the caramelized onions. Repeat with the remaining Spätzle mixture and caramelized onions.
7. Bake the Käsespätzle in the preheated oven for 15-20 minutes, or until the cheese is melted and bubbly.
8. While the Käsespätzle is baking, prepare the salad. In a large bowl, toss together the mixed greens, cherry tomatoes, sliced cucumber, and thinly sliced red onion. Drizzle with your favorite salad dressing and toss to coat.
9. Once the Käsespätzle is done baking, remove it from the oven and let it cool slightly. Garnish with chopped fresh parsley if desired.
10. Serve the Käsespätzle hot alongside the salad.
11. Enjoy your delicious Käsespätzle with Caramelized Onions and Salad, a comforting and satisfying German meal!

Erbsensuppe (Pea Soup) with Wiener Wurstchen

Ingredients:

For the Erbsensuppe:

- 2 tablespoons butter or oil
- 1 onion, chopped
- 2 carrots, diced
- 2 celery stalks, diced
- 2 cloves garlic, minced
- 1 lb dried split peas, rinsed and drained
- 8 cups chicken or vegetable broth
- 2 bay leaves
- 1 teaspoon dried thyme
- Salt and pepper to taste
- 1 cup diced cooked ham (optional, for extra flavor)

For serving:

- Wiener Würstchen (Vienna sausages), sliced
- Chopped fresh parsley for garnish (optional)

Instructions:

1. In a large pot or Dutch oven, heat the butter or oil over medium heat. Add the chopped onion, diced carrots, and diced celery. Cook, stirring occasionally, until the vegetables are softened, about 5-7 minutes.
2. Add the minced garlic to the pot and cook for an additional 1-2 minutes, until fragrant.
3. Stir in the dried split peas, chicken or vegetable broth, bay leaves, and dried thyme. Bring the mixture to a boil, then reduce the heat to low.
4. Cover the pot and let the soup simmer for about 1 hour, stirring occasionally, or until the split peas are soft and tender.
5. If using, add the diced cooked ham to the soup and let it simmer for an additional 10-15 minutes to heat through.

6. Once the split peas are cooked and the soup has thickened, remove the bay leaves from the pot. Season the soup with salt and pepper to taste.
7. Ladle the Erbsensuppe into bowls and top each serving with sliced Wiener Würstchen.
8. Garnish with chopped fresh parsley if desired.
9. Serve the Erbsensuppe hot and enjoy your delicious and comforting pea soup with Wiener Würstchen!

Feel free to adjust the thickness of the soup by adding more broth if desired. You can also customize the flavor by adding different herbs or spices to suit your taste.

Gulaschsuppe (Goulash Soup) with Bread

Ingredients:

For the Gulaschsuppe:

- 2 tablespoons vegetable oil
- 1 onion, chopped
- 2 cloves garlic, minced
- 1 lb beef stew meat, cut into bite-sized pieces
- 2 tablespoons sweet paprika
- 1 teaspoon caraway seeds
- 1 teaspoon dried thyme
- 2 tablespoons tomato paste
- 4 cups beef broth
- 1 cup diced tomatoes (canned or fresh)
- 2 potatoes, peeled and diced
- Salt and pepper to taste
- Chopped fresh parsley for garnish (optional)

For serving:

- Slices of crusty bread or bread rolls

Instructions:

1. Heat the vegetable oil in a large pot or Dutch oven over medium heat. Add the chopped onion and minced garlic and cook until softened, about 5 minutes.
2. Add the beef stew meat to the pot and cook until browned on all sides, about 5-7 minutes.
3. Stir in the sweet paprika, caraway seeds, dried thyme, and tomato paste. Cook for another 2-3 minutes to toast the spices and tomato paste.
4. Pour in the beef broth and diced tomatoes, stirring to combine. Bring the mixture to a simmer.
5. Add the diced potatoes to the pot and season the soup with salt and pepper to taste.

6. Cover the pot and let the Gulaschsuppe simmer for about 1 hour, stirring occasionally, or until the beef is tender and the potatoes are cooked through.
7. Taste and adjust the seasoning if necessary.
8. Ladle the Gulaschsuppe into bowls and garnish with chopped fresh parsley if desired.
9. Serve the Gulaschsuppe hot, accompanied by slices of crusty bread or bread rolls for dipping.
10. Enjoy your delicious and comforting Gulaschsuppe with bread, a perfect meal for chilly days!

Wurstsalat with German Bread

Ingredients:

For the Wurstsalat:

- 8 oz German sausage (such as Bockwurst, Weisswurst, or Fleischwurst), thinly sliced
- 1 small onion, thinly sliced
- 1 dill pickle, thinly sliced
- 2 tablespoons chopped fresh parsley
- 2 tablespoons white wine vinegar
- 1 tablespoon olive oil
- 1 teaspoon mustard
- Salt and pepper to taste

For serving:

- Slices of German bread (such as Vollkornbrot, Roggenbrot, or Bauernbrot)

Instructions:

1. In a large bowl, combine the thinly sliced sausage, onion, pickle, and chopped parsley.
2. In a small bowl, whisk together the white wine vinegar, olive oil, mustard, salt, and pepper to make the vinaigrette.
3. Pour the vinaigrette over the sausage mixture and toss to coat everything evenly.
4. Cover the bowl and let the Wurstsalat marinate in the refrigerator for at least 30 minutes to allow the flavors to meld together.
5. Before serving, give the Wurstsalat a final toss and taste for seasoning, adding more salt and pepper if needed.
6. Serve the Wurstsalat chilled, accompanied by slices of German bread.
7. Enjoy your delicious Wurstsalat with German bread, a perfect combination of flavors and textures that's sure to satisfy your cravings!

Bauernfrühstück (German Farmer's Breakfast) with Bread

Ingredients:

- 4 slices bacon or ham, diced
- 4 medium potatoes, peeled and diced
- 1 onion, chopped
- 4 eggs
- Salt and pepper to taste
- Chopped fresh parsley for garnish (optional)
- Slices of crusty bread

Instructions:

1. In a large skillet, cook the diced bacon or ham over medium heat until it's crispy and the fat has rendered out.
2. Remove the cooked bacon or ham from the skillet and set it aside, leaving the rendered fat in the skillet.
3. Add the diced potatoes to the skillet with the rendered fat. Cook the potatoes, stirring occasionally, until they are golden brown and crispy on the outside and tender on the inside. This will take about 10-15 minutes.
4. Add the chopped onion to the skillet with the potatoes and cook until the onion is soft and translucent, about 5 minutes.
5. Return the cooked bacon or ham to the skillet and stir to combine everything evenly.
6. Make four wells in the potato mixture with the back of a spoon. Crack an egg into each well.
7. Season the eggs with salt and pepper to taste. Cover the skillet and cook until the eggs are cooked to your desired doneness. For runny yolks, this will take about 3-5 minutes.
8. While the eggs are cooking, toast the slices of crusty bread until they're golden brown and crispy.
9. Once the eggs are cooked, remove the skillet from the heat and garnish the Bauernfrühstück with chopped fresh parsley if desired.
10. Serve the Bauernfrühstück hot, accompanied by slices of crusty bread for dipping and mopping up the delicious runny yolks.

11. Enjoy your hearty and delicious Bauernfrühstück with crusty bread, a classic German breakfast that's sure to keep you satisfied all morning!

Kartoffelsuppe (Potato Soup) with Croutons

Ingredients:

For the Potato Soup:

- 2 tablespoons butter or olive oil
- 1 onion, chopped
- 2 cloves garlic, minced
- 4 cups potatoes, peeled and diced
- 4 cups vegetable or chicken broth
- 1 cup milk or cream
- Salt and pepper to taste
- Chopped fresh parsley or chives for garnish (optional)

For the Croutons:

- 4 slices bread, cut into cubes
- 2 tablespoons olive oil
- 1 teaspoon garlic powder
- 1 teaspoon dried thyme
- Salt and pepper to taste

Instructions:

For the Potato Soup:

1. In a large pot or Dutch oven, heat the butter or olive oil over medium heat. Add the chopped onion and minced garlic and cook until softened, about 5 minutes.
2. Add the diced potatoes to the pot and cook for another 5 minutes, stirring occasionally.
3. Pour in the vegetable or chicken broth and bring the mixture to a boil. Reduce the heat to low and let the soup simmer for about 15-20 minutes, or until the potatoes are tender.

4. Using an immersion blender or countertop blender, puree the soup until smooth. If using a countertop blender, work in batches and be careful not to overfill the blender with hot liquid.
5. Stir in the milk or cream and season the soup with salt and pepper to taste. Let the soup simmer for another 5-10 minutes to heat through.
6. While the soup is simmering, prepare the croutons.

For the Croutons:

1. Preheat your oven to 375°F (190°C).
2. In a large bowl, toss the bread cubes with olive oil, garlic powder, dried thyme, salt, and pepper until evenly coated.
3. Spread the seasoned bread cubes in a single layer on a baking sheet.
4. Bake the croutons in the preheated oven for 10-15 minutes, or until golden brown and crispy, stirring occasionally to ensure even browning.
5. Remove the croutons from the oven and let them cool slightly before serving.

To serve:

1. Ladle the hot Kartoffelsuppe into bowls.
2. Top each serving of soup with a handful of crispy croutons.
3. Garnish with chopped fresh parsley or chives if desired.
4. Serve the Kartoffelsuppe with croutons hot and enjoy your delicious and comforting potato soup!

Käsefondue (Cheese Fondue) with Bread and Pickles

Ingredients:

For the Cheese Fondue:

- 1 clove garlic, peeled and halved
- 1 cup dry white wine
- 1 tablespoon lemon juice
- 1/2 lb Emmental cheese, grated
- 1/2 lb Gruyère cheese, grated
- 2 tablespoons cornstarch
- 2 tablespoons kirsch (optional)
- Salt, pepper, and nutmeg to taste

For serving:

- Cubes of crusty bread
- Assorted pickles (gherkins, cocktail onions, etc.)
- Cubes of cooked ham or sausage (optional)
- Cubes of vegetables (bell peppers, cherry tomatoes, etc.)

Instructions:

1. Rub the inside of a fondue pot with the halved garlic clove.
2. In a saucepan, heat the white wine and lemon juice over medium heat until it simmers.
3. In a bowl, toss the grated Emmental and Gruyère cheeses with the cornstarch until the cheese is coated.
4. Gradually add the cheese mixture to the simmering wine, stirring constantly in a figure-eight motion until the cheese is melted and smooth.
5. Stir in the kirsch (if using) and season the fondue with salt, pepper, and nutmeg to taste.
6. Transfer the fondue pot to the fondue burner and keep the cheese mixture warm over low heat.

7. Arrange the bread cubes, pickles, cooked ham or sausage (if using), and vegetable cubes on a serving platter.
8. To serve, spear a piece of bread or other accompaniment with a fondue fork and dip it into the melted cheese, swirling to coat. Be careful not to drip cheese into the fondue pot.
9. Enjoy your Käsefondue with bread and pickles, savoring each flavorful dip! Remember to stir the cheese mixture occasionally to prevent it from scorching.

Bratwurst with Potato Salad and Mustard

Ingredients:

For the Bratwurst:

- 4 bratwurst sausages
- 1 tablespoon vegetable oil

For the Potato Salad:

- 1 lb potatoes (preferably waxy varieties like Yukon Gold or red potatoes)
- 1/4 cup finely chopped red onion
- 2 tablespoons chopped fresh parsley
- 2 tablespoons apple cider vinegar
- 2 tablespoons olive oil
- 1 tablespoon Dijon mustard
- Salt and pepper to taste

For serving:

- Dijon mustard for dipping
- Additional chopped fresh parsley for garnish (optional)

Instructions:

1. Start by preparing the potato salad. Peel the potatoes and cut them into bite-sized pieces. Place them in a pot of salted water and bring to a boil. Cook until the potatoes are fork-tender, about 10-15 minutes. Drain and let cool slightly.
2. In a large bowl, whisk together the apple cider vinegar, olive oil, Dijon mustard, salt, and pepper to make the dressing.
3. Add the chopped red onion and parsley to the dressing and stir to combine.
4. Add the cooked potatoes to the bowl and gently toss until they are evenly coated with the dressing. Adjust seasoning if necessary. Set aside.
5. Preheat a grill or grill pan over medium-high heat. Brush the bratwurst sausages with vegetable oil to prevent sticking.

6. Grill the bratwurst sausages until they are browned and cooked through, turning occasionally, about 10-12 minutes.
7. While the sausages are grilling, you can also warm the potato salad slightly if desired.
8. Once the sausages are cooked, remove them from the grill and serve hot alongside the potato salad.
9. Serve the bratwurst with potato salad and Dijon mustard on the side for dipping.
10. Garnish with additional chopped parsley if desired.
11. Enjoy your delicious bratwurst with potato salad and mustard, a classic German meal that's sure to please!

Labskaus with Fried Egg and Pickled Herring

Ingredients:

For the Labskaus:

- 1 lb salted beef or corned beef
- 1 lb potatoes
- 2 onions, finely chopped
- 2 large beets, cooked and diced
- 4 tablespoons butter
- Salt and pepper to taste

For serving:

- Fried eggs
- Pickled herring fillets
- Chopped fresh parsley for garnish (optional)
- Rye bread or other hearty bread, for serving

Instructions:

1. Start by soaking the salted beef in cold water for several hours or overnight to remove excess salt. Change the water a few times during soaking.
2. Peel and dice the potatoes, then boil them in salted water until tender. Drain and set aside.
3. In a large skillet, melt 2 tablespoons of butter over medium heat. Add the chopped onions and cook until soft and translucent, about 5-7 minutes.
4. Add the diced beets to the skillet and cook for another 5 minutes, stirring occasionally.
5. Meanwhile, drain the soaked salted beef and place it in a large pot. Cover with water and bring to a boil. Reduce the heat and simmer until the beef is cooked through and tender, about 1-2 hours.
6. Once the beef is cooked, drain it and shred it using two forks or chop it finely.
7. Add the cooked potatoes to the pot with the shredded beef. Mash everything together with a potato masher or fork until well combined.

8. Add the cooked onions and beets to the pot with the beef and potatoes. Stir to combine.
9. Season the Labskaus with salt and pepper to taste.
10. In a separate skillet, melt the remaining 2 tablespoons of butter over medium heat. Crack the eggs into the skillet and fry them until the whites are set but the yolks are still runny.
11. To serve, divide the Labskaus among serving plates. Top each portion with a fried egg and a pickled herring fillet.
12. Garnish with chopped fresh parsley if desired.
13. Serve the Labskaus hot with rye bread or other hearty bread on the side.

Enjoy your Labskaus with fried egg and pickled herring, a traditional and hearty Northern German dish!

Grünkohl with Mettwurst and Boiled Potatoes

Ingredients:

For the Grünkohl:

- 2 lbs fresh kale (Grünkohl), washed and chopped
- 1 onion, finely chopped
- 2 cloves garlic, minced
- 4 slices bacon, diced
- 1 tablespoon vegetable oil
- 1 cup chicken or vegetable broth
- 1 bay leaf
- Salt and pepper to taste
- Pinch of nutmeg (optional)
- 1-2 tablespoons apple cider vinegar or white vinegar (optional, for added tanginess)

For serving:

- Mettwurst or any German sausage of your choice, sliced
- Boiled potatoes

Instructions:

1. In a large pot or Dutch oven, heat the vegetable oil over medium heat. Add the diced bacon and cook until it starts to render its fat and becomes crispy.
2. Add the chopped onion to the pot and cook until it's soft and translucent, about 5-7 minutes.
3. Stir in the minced garlic and cook for another 1-2 minutes, until fragrant.
4. Add the chopped kale to the pot, along with the chicken or vegetable broth and bay leaf. Stir well to combine.
5. Season the kale mixture with salt, pepper, and a pinch of nutmeg if using. You can also add a splash of apple cider vinegar or white vinegar for added tanginess if desired.

6. Cover the pot and let the kale mixture simmer over low heat for about 30-40 minutes, stirring occasionally, until the kale is tender and cooked through.
7. While the kale is simmering, prepare the boiled potatoes by washing them and boiling them in salted water until they're fork-tender. Drain and set aside.
8. Once the kale is cooked, taste and adjust the seasoning if necessary.
9. Serve the Grünkohl hot, alongside sliced Mettwurst and boiled potatoes.
10. Enjoy your hearty and delicious Grünkohl with Mettwurst and boiled potatoes, a classic German dish that's perfect for a comforting meal!

Kartoffelpuffer (Potato Pancakes) with Applesauce

Ingredients:

For the Kartoffelpuffer:

- 4 large potatoes, peeled
- 1 small onion
- 1 egg
- 2 tablespoons all-purpose flour
- 1/2 teaspoon salt
- 1/4 teaspoon black pepper
- Vegetable oil for frying

For serving:

- Applesauce
- Sour cream or Greek yogurt (optional)
- Chopped fresh chives or parsley for garnish (optional)

Instructions:

1. Grate the peeled potatoes and onion using a box grater or a food processor fitted with a grating attachment. Place the grated potatoes and onion in a clean kitchen towel or cheesecloth and squeeze out as much moisture as possible.
2. Transfer the squeezed potatoes and onion to a mixing bowl. Add the egg, flour, salt, and black pepper, and mix until well combined.
3. Heat a thin layer of vegetable oil in a large skillet over medium heat.
4. Once the oil is hot, drop spoonfuls of the potato mixture into the skillet, flattening them slightly with the back of a spoon to form pancakes.
5. Fry the Kartoffelpuffer for 3-4 minutes on each side, or until golden brown and crispy. You may need to fry them in batches, adding more oil to the skillet as needed.
6. Transfer the cooked Kartoffelpuffer to a plate lined with paper towels to drain any excess oil.

7. Serve the Kartoffelpuffer hot, with a dollop of applesauce on top. If desired, you can also serve them with a side of sour cream or Greek yogurt for dipping.
8. Garnish with chopped fresh chives or parsley if desired.
9. Enjoy your delicious Kartoffelpuffer with applesauce, a classic German treat that's perfect for any occasion!

Maultaschen Soup with Bread

Ingredients:

For the Maultaschen:

- 8 Maultaschen (store-bought or homemade)
- 6 cups chicken or vegetable broth

For the soup:

- 2 tablespoons butter or olive oil
- 1 onion, diced
- 2 carrots, diced
- 2 celery stalks, diced
- 2 cloves garlic, minced
- 6 cups chicken or vegetable broth
- Salt and pepper to taste
- Chopped fresh parsley for garnish (optional)

For serving:

- Slices of crusty bread or bread rolls

Instructions:

1. In a large pot, heat the butter or olive oil over medium heat. Add the diced onion, carrots, and celery. Cook until the vegetables are softened, about 5-7 minutes.
2. Add the minced garlic to the pot and cook for an additional 1-2 minutes, until fragrant.
3. Pour in the chicken or vegetable broth and bring the soup to a simmer. Let it simmer for about 10 minutes to allow the flavors to meld together.

4. While the soup is simmering, bring another pot of water to a boil. Add the Maultaschen and cook according to the package instructions, usually about 8-10 minutes. Drain and set aside.
5. Once the soup has simmered and the vegetables are tender, season it with salt and pepper to taste.
6. To serve, ladle the soup into bowls and add a few cooked Maultaschen to each bowl.
7. Garnish with chopped fresh parsley if desired.
8. Serve the Maultaschen soup hot, accompanied by slices of crusty bread or bread rolls for dipping.
9. Enjoy your comforting Maultaschen soup with bread, a delicious and satisfying meal!

Käsespätzle with Roasted Onions and Salad

Ingredients:

For the Spätzle:

- 2 cups all-purpose flour
- 4 large eggs
- 1/2 cup milk
- 1/2 teaspoon salt
- 1/4 teaspoon freshly grated nutmeg

For the Cheese Sauce:

- 2 tablespoons butter
- 2 tablespoons all-purpose flour
- 2 cups milk
- 2 cups shredded Emmental cheese (or any other Swiss cheese)
- Salt and pepper to taste

For the Roasted Onions:

- 2 large onions, thinly sliced
- 2 tablespoons olive oil
- Salt and pepper to taste

For the Salad:

- Mixed greens
- Cherry tomatoes, halved
- Cucumber, sliced
- Red onion, thinly sliced
- Balsamic vinaigrette or your favorite dressing

Instructions:

1. Preheat the oven to 400°F (200°C). Line a baking sheet with parchment paper.
2. In a large bowl, whisk together the flour, eggs, milk, salt, and nutmeg until you have a smooth, thick batter.
3. Bring a large pot of salted water to a boil. Place a spätzle maker or colander over the pot and press the batter through the holes into the boiling water. Alternatively, you can use a spoon to drop small amounts of batter into the water.
4. Cook the spätzle for about 2-3 minutes, or until they float to the surface. Remove them with a slotted spoon and transfer to a colander to drain.
5. In a large skillet, heat the olive oil over medium heat. Add the sliced onions and cook, stirring occasionally, until they are caramelized and golden brown, about 15-20 minutes. Season with salt and pepper to taste.
6. In a separate saucepan, melt the butter over medium heat. Stir in the flour and cook for 1-2 minutes, until golden brown.
7. Gradually whisk in the milk, stirring constantly to prevent lumps from forming. Cook until the sauce thickens, about 5-7 minutes.
8. Stir in the shredded cheese until melted and smooth. Season with salt and pepper to taste.
9. Add the cooked spätzle to the cheese sauce and toss to coat evenly.
10. Transfer the cheesy spätzle to the prepared baking sheet. Spread the caramelized onions over the top.
11. Bake in the preheated oven for 15-20 minutes, or until the top is golden brown and bubbly.
12. While the Käsespätzle is baking, prepare the salad by tossing together the mixed greens, cherry tomatoes, cucumber, and red onion. Drizzle with your favorite dressing.
13. Serve the Käsespätzle hot, with the salad on the side.

Enjoy your delicious Käsespätzle with roasted onions and salad!

Senfbraten (Mustard Roast) with Red Cabbage and Potato Dumplings

Ingredients:

For the Senfbraten:

- 2 lbs pork loin or beef roast
- 1/4 cup Dijon mustard
- 2 tablespoons whole grain mustard
- 2 cloves garlic, minced
- 2 tablespoons olive oil
- Salt and pepper to taste

For the Red Cabbage:

- 1 small red cabbage, thinly sliced
- 1 onion, thinly sliced
- 2 tablespoons butter
- 2 tablespoons red wine vinegar
- 2 tablespoons brown sugar
- Salt and pepper to taste

For the Potato Dumplings:

- 2 lbs potatoes, peeled and quartered
- 1 cup all-purpose flour
- 2 eggs
- Salt and pepper to taste
- Butter for serving

Instructions:

1. Preheat the oven to 350°F (175°C).

2. In a small bowl, mix together the Dijon mustard, whole grain mustard, minced garlic, olive oil, salt, and pepper to make the marinade.
3. Rub the marinade all over the pork loin or beef roast, ensuring it's evenly coated. Let it marinate for at least 30 minutes, or ideally overnight in the refrigerator.
4. Place the marinated meat in a roasting pan and roast in the preheated oven for about 1 to 1.5 hours, or until the internal temperature reaches 145°F (63°C) for pork or 135°F (57°C) for beef. Remove from the oven and let it rest for 10 minutes before slicing.
5. While the meat is roasting, prepare the red cabbage. In a large skillet or Dutch oven, melt the butter over medium heat. Add the sliced onion and cook until softened, about 5 minutes.
6. Add the sliced red cabbage to the skillet and cook, stirring occasionally, until it starts to wilt, about 5-7 minutes.
7. Stir in the red wine vinegar and brown sugar. Season with salt and pepper to taste. Cover and simmer for about 30-40 minutes, or until the cabbage is tender.
8. Meanwhile, prepare the potato dumplings. Boil the potatoes in salted water until tender, about 15-20 minutes. Drain and let cool slightly.
9. Mash the boiled potatoes until smooth. Add the flour, eggs, salt, and pepper, and mix until well combined.
10. Shape the potato mixture into dumplings, about the size of golf balls.
11. Bring a large pot of salted water to a boil. Carefully drop the potato dumplings into the boiling water and cook for about 10-12 minutes, or until they float to the surface.
12. Serve the sliced Senfbraten with red cabbage and potato dumplings. Garnish with butter and serve hot.

Enjoy your delicious Senfbraten with red cabbage and potato dumplings, a hearty and satisfying German meal!

Wurstsalat with Pretzel and Radishes

Ingredients:

For the Wurstsalat:

- 1/2 lb German sausage (such as Fleischwurst, Lyoner, or Bologna), thinly sliced
- 1 small red onion, thinly sliced
- 1 small cucumber, thinly sliced
- 4-6 radishes, thinly sliced
- 2 tablespoons white wine vinegar
- 1 tablespoon olive oil
- 1 teaspoon mustard
- 1 teaspoon honey or sugar
- Salt and pepper to taste
- Chopped fresh parsley for garnish (optional)

For serving:

- Pretzels, sliced
- Additional radishes, sliced

Instructions:

1. In a large bowl, combine the sliced German sausage, red onion, cucumber, and radishes.
2. In a small bowl, whisk together the white wine vinegar, olive oil, mustard, honey or sugar, salt, and pepper to make the dressing.
3. Pour the dressing over the sausage and vegetable mixture. Toss until everything is well coated.
4. Cover the bowl and refrigerate the Wurstsalat for at least 30 minutes to allow the flavors to meld together.
5. Just before serving, garnish the Wurstsalat with chopped fresh parsley if desired.
6. Serve the Wurstsalat with sliced pretzels and additional radishes on the side.
7. Enjoy your delicious Wurstsalat with pretzel and radishes as a light meal or appetizer!

This dish is perfect for a picnic, barbecue, or casual gathering with friends and family. The combination of flavors and textures makes it a true delight to enjoy.

Leberwurstbrot (Liverwurst Sandwich) with Pickles

Ingredients:

- Slices of bread (rye bread, whole grain bread, or your favorite sandwich bread)
- Liverwurst (German liver sausage)
- Pickles, sliced
- Mustard (optional)
- Fresh parsley or chives for garnish (optional)

Instructions:

1. Toast the slices of bread until they are golden brown and crispy, if desired.
2. Spread a generous amount of liverwurst onto each slice of bread. You can use a knife or a small spatula to spread it evenly.
3. Place several slices of pickles on top of the liverwurst. You can adjust the amount of pickles according to your preference.
4. If desired, add a dollop of mustard on top of the pickles for an extra kick of flavor.
5. Garnish the Leberwurstbrot with fresh parsley or chives for a pop of color and freshness, if desired.
6. Serve the Leberwurstbrot immediately, either as an open-faced sandwich or topped with another slice of bread to make it a traditional sandwich.
7. Enjoy your delicious Leberwurstbrot with pickles as a quick and satisfying snack or light meal!

This simple recipe allows you to enjoy the rich and savory flavors of liverwurst paired with the tangy crunch of pickles, all sandwiched between slices of hearty bread. It's a classic German treat that's sure to satisfy your taste buds.

Semmelknödel (Bread Dumplings) with Mushroom Sauce and Salad

Ingredients:

For the Semmelknödel:

- 6 large bread rolls or buns (preferably stale)
- 1 onion, finely chopped
- 2 cloves garlic, minced
- 3 tablespoons butter
- 1 cup milk
- 3 eggs
- Salt, pepper, and nutmeg to taste
- Chopped parsley for garnish

For the Mushroom Sauce:

- 2 tablespoons butter
- 1 onion, finely chopped
- 8 oz mushrooms, sliced
- 2 cloves garlic, minced
- 2 tablespoons all-purpose flour
- 1 cup vegetable or chicken broth
- 1/2 cup heavy cream
- Salt and pepper to taste
- Chopped fresh parsley for garnish

For the Salad:

- Mixed greens
- Cherry tomatoes, halved
- Cucumber, sliced
- Red onion, thinly sliced
- Balsamic vinaigrette or your favorite dressing

Instructions:

1. Begin by preparing the Semmelknödel. Cut the bread rolls into small cubes and place them in a large mixing bowl.
2. In a skillet, melt 2 tablespoons of butter over medium heat. Add the chopped onion and garlic, and sauté until softened, about 5 minutes. Remove from heat and let cool slightly.
3. In a separate saucepan, heat the milk until warm but not boiling. Pour the warm milk over the bread cubes and let them soak for about 10 minutes.
4. Once the bread cubes have soaked up the milk, add the sautéed onion and garlic mixture to the bowl. Also, add the eggs, salt, pepper, and a pinch of nutmeg. Mix everything together until well combined.
5. With damp hands, form the bread mixture into golf ball-sized dumplings.
6. Bring a large pot of salted water to a gentle simmer. Carefully drop the dumplings into the water and simmer for about 15-20 minutes, or until they are cooked through. They should float to the surface when done.
7. While the dumplings are cooking, prepare the mushroom sauce. In a skillet, melt 2 tablespoons of butter over medium heat. Add the chopped onion and cook until softened, about 5 minutes. Add the sliced mushrooms and minced garlic, and cook until the mushrooms are golden brown and tender, about 8-10 minutes.
8. Sprinkle the flour over the mushrooms and stir to coat. Cook for 1-2 minutes, then gradually whisk in the vegetable or chicken broth. Bring the mixture to a simmer and cook until thickened, about 5 minutes. Stir in the heavy cream and season with salt and pepper to taste.
9. For the salad, toss together mixed greens, cherry tomatoes, cucumber, and red onion in a large bowl. Drizzle with balsamic vinaigrette or your favorite dressing.
10. Once the Semmelknödel are cooked, remove them from the pot with a slotted spoon and drain on a plate lined with paper towels.
11. To serve, spoon the mushroom sauce over the Semmelknödel and garnish with chopped parsley. Serve with the salad on the side.
12. Enjoy your delicious Semmelknödel with mushroom sauce and salad!

This hearty and satisfying meal is perfect for brunch or a cozy dinner at home. The Semmelknödel are soft and pillowy, while the creamy mushroom sauce adds richness and depth of flavor.

Sauerbraten with Potato Pancakes and Red Cabbage

Ingredients:

For the Sauerbraten:

- 3-4 pounds beef roast (such as chuck or round)
- 1 cup red wine vinegar
- 1 cup water
- 1 onion, sliced
- 2 carrots, sliced
- 2 celery stalks, sliced
- 2 cloves garlic, minced
- 2 bay leaves
- 6 whole cloves
- 6 whole peppercorns
- 1 tablespoon sugar
- Salt and pepper to taste
- 2 tablespoons vegetable oil
- 2 tablespoons all-purpose flour
- 1 cup beef broth

For the Potato Pancakes:

- 4 large potatoes, peeled and grated
- 1 onion, grated
- 2 eggs
- 2 tablespoons all-purpose flour
- Salt and pepper to taste
- Vegetable oil for frying

For the Red Cabbage:

- 1 small head of red cabbage, shredded
- 1 onion, sliced
- 2 apples, peeled, cored, and sliced

- 1/4 cup red wine vinegar
- 1/4 cup apple cider vinegar
- 1/4 cup brown sugar
- 1/2 teaspoon ground cloves
- Salt and pepper to taste

Instructions:

1. To prepare the Sauerbraten, place the beef roast in a large resealable plastic bag. In a mixing bowl, combine the red wine vinegar, water, sliced onion, carrots, celery, minced garlic, bay leaves, whole cloves, whole peppercorns, sugar, salt, and pepper. Pour the marinade over the beef roast, seal the bag, and refrigerate overnight, turning occasionally.
2. Preheat the oven to 325°F (160°C).
3. Remove the beef roast from the marinade and pat it dry with paper towels. Strain the marinade and reserve the liquid and vegetables.
4. In a Dutch oven or large oven-safe pot, heat the vegetable oil over medium-high heat. Sear the beef roast on all sides until browned, about 5 minutes per side. Remove the roast from the pot and set aside.
5. Add the reserved vegetables from the marinade to the pot and cook until softened, about 5 minutes. Sprinkle the flour over the vegetables and cook for an additional 1-2 minutes.
6. Return the beef roast to the pot and pour in the reserved marinade liquid and beef broth. Cover the pot with a lid and transfer it to the preheated oven. Cook for 3-4 hours, or until the beef is tender and falling apart.
7. While the Sauerbraten is cooking, prepare the Potato Pancakes. In a large mixing bowl, combine the grated potatoes, grated onion, eggs, flour, salt, and pepper. Mix until well combined.
8. Heat a thin layer of vegetable oil in a large skillet over medium heat. Drop spoonfuls of the potato mixture into the skillet and flatten them with the back of a spoon to form pancakes. Cook until golden brown and crispy on both sides, about 3-4 minutes per side. Transfer the cooked pancakes to a plate lined with paper towels to drain.
9. For the Red Cabbage, heat a tablespoon of vegetable oil in a large skillet or Dutch oven over medium heat. Add the sliced onion and cook until softened, about 5 minutes. Add the shredded red cabbage and sliced apples to the skillet.

10. In a small bowl, mix together the red wine vinegar, apple cider vinegar, brown sugar, ground cloves, salt, and pepper. Pour the vinegar mixture over the red cabbage and apples. Stir to combine.
11. Cover the skillet and cook the red cabbage over medium heat, stirring occasionally, until tender, about 30-40 minutes.
12. Once the Sauerbraten is done cooking, remove it from the oven and let it rest for a few minutes before slicing.
13. Serve the Sauerbraten slices with Potato Pancakes and Red Cabbage on the side.
14. Enjoy your delicious Sauerbraten with Potato Pancakes and Red Cabbage, a comforting and flavorful German meal!

This meal is perfect for special occasions or Sunday dinners with family and friends.

The tender and tangy Sauerbraten pairs beautifully with the crispy Potato Pancakes and sweet-sour Red Cabbage, creating a memorable dining experience.

Wurstsalat with German Bread and Pickles

Ingredients:

For the Wurstsalat:

- 1 lb German sausage (such as Fleischwurst, Lyoner, or Bologna), thinly sliced
- 1 small red onion, thinly sliced
- 1 small cucumber, thinly sliced
- 4-6 pickles, thinly sliced
- 2 tablespoons white wine vinegar
- 1 tablespoon apple cider vinegar
- 2 tablespoons olive oil
- 1 teaspoon mustard
- 1 teaspoon honey or sugar
- Salt and pepper to taste
- Chopped fresh parsley for garnish (optional)

For serving:

- German bread (such as rye bread or pretzel rolls)
- Additional pickles for garnish

Instructions:

1. In a large mixing bowl, combine the thinly sliced German sausage, red onion, cucumber, and pickles.
2. In a small bowl, whisk together the white wine vinegar, apple cider vinegar, olive oil, mustard, honey or sugar, salt, and pepper to make the dressing.
3. Pour the dressing over the Wurstsalat mixture and toss until everything is well coated.
4. Cover the bowl and refrigerate the Wurstsalat for at least 30 minutes to allow the flavors to meld together.
5. Just before serving, garnish the Wurstsalat with chopped fresh parsley, if desired.
6. Serve the Wurstsalat with slices of German bread and additional pickles on the side.

7. Enjoy your delicious Wurstsalat with German bread and pickles as a light meal or appetizer!

This dish is perfect for picnics, potlucks, or casual gatherings with friends and family. The combination of flavors and textures is sure to be a hit, and it pairs wonderfully with crusty German bread and crunchy pickles.

Labskaus with Rollmops and Pickled Beetroot

Ingredients:

For the Labskaus:

- 1 lb corned beef or salted meat
- 4 large potatoes
- 2 onions
- 2 tablespoons butter
- Salt and pepper to taste
- 4 eggs (optional)
- Pickled beetroot for serving
- Rollmops (pickled herring fillets) for serving

Instructions:

1. Peel the potatoes and cut them into small cubes. Peel and finely chop the onions.
2. In a large pot, cover the corned beef or salted meat with water and bring to a boil. Reduce the heat and simmer for about 1-2 hours, or until the meat is tender.
3. While the meat is cooking, boil the potatoes in a separate pot of salted water until tender, about 15-20 minutes. Drain and set aside.
4. In a skillet, melt the butter over medium heat. Add the chopped onions and cook until softened and translucent, about 5-7 minutes.
5. Once the meat is cooked, remove it from the pot and shred it using two forks.
6. In a large mixing bowl, combine the shredded meat, cooked potatoes, and sautéed onions. Season with salt and pepper to taste. Mix everything together until well combined.
7. To serve, divide the Labskaus onto individual plates. If desired, fry an egg for each serving and place it on top of the Labskaus.
8. Serve the Labskaus with pickled beetroot and Rollmops on the side.
9. Enjoy your delicious Labskaus with Rollmops and Pickled Beetroot!

This hearty and flavorful dish is perfect for a traditional Northern German meal. The combination of tender corned beef, creamy potatoes, and savory onions, paired with the tangy pickled beetroot and Rollmops, creates a unique and satisfying dining experience.

Erbseneintopf (Split Pea Soup) with Frankfurters

Ingredients:

For the Split Pea Soup:

- 2 cups dried split peas, rinsed and drained
- 1 onion, chopped
- 2 carrots, chopped
- 2 celery stalks, chopped
- 2 cloves garlic, minced
- 6 cups chicken or vegetable broth
- 2 bay leaves
- Salt and pepper to taste

For serving:

- Frankfurters or Wiener sausages
- Chopped fresh parsley for garnish (optional)
- Crusty bread or rolls

Instructions:

1. In a large pot, heat a bit of oil over medium heat. Add the chopped onion, carrots, celery, and garlic. Cook, stirring occasionally, until the vegetables are softened, about 5-7 minutes.
2. Add the rinsed split peas to the pot, along with the chicken or vegetable broth and bay leaves. Bring the mixture to a boil, then reduce the heat to low and simmer, partially covered, for about 1 to 1 1/2 hours, or until the peas are tender and the soup has thickened, stirring occasionally.
3. Once the soup has reached the desired consistency, remove the bay leaves and season with salt and pepper to taste.
4. While the soup is simmering, prepare the Frankfurters according to package instructions. You can boil them, grill them, or pan-fry them until heated through.
5. To serve, ladle the hot split pea soup into bowls. Slice the Frankfurters and add them to the bowls of soup. Garnish with chopped fresh parsley if desired.

6. Serve the split pea soup with Frankfurters alongside crusty bread or rolls for dipping.
7. Enjoy your delicious Erbseneintopf with Frankfurters, a comforting and satisfying meal for any day of the week!

This classic German dish is easy to make and packed with flavor. The combination of tender split peas, aromatic vegetables, and savory Frankfurters makes for a comforting and nutritious meal that's sure to warm you up on a chilly day.

Gulaschsuppe with Rye Bread

Ingredients:

For the Gulaschsuppe:

- 1 lb beef stew meat, cut into bite-sized pieces
- 2 tablespoons vegetable oil
- 1 onion, diced
- 2 cloves garlic, minced
- 2 tablespoons sweet paprika
- 1 teaspoon caraway seeds
- 1 teaspoon dried thyme
- 1 bay leaf
- Salt and pepper to taste
- 4 cups beef broth
- 1 cup diced tomatoes (canned or fresh)
- 2 potatoes, peeled and diced
- 1 carrot, peeled and diced
- 1 bell pepper, diced
- 1/2 cup red wine (optional)
- Chopped fresh parsley for garnish

For serving:

- Rye bread, sliced

Instructions:

1. In a large pot or Dutch oven, heat the vegetable oil over medium-high heat. Add the diced onion and cook until softened, about 5 minutes. Add the minced garlic and cook for an additional 1-2 minutes.
2. Add the beef stew meat to the pot and cook until browned on all sides, about 5-7 minutes.
3. Stir in the sweet paprika, caraway seeds, dried thyme, bay leaf, salt, and pepper, and cook for another minute to toast the spices.

4. Pour in the beef broth and diced tomatoes, and bring the mixture to a simmer. Cover the pot and cook for about 1 hour, or until the meat is tender.
5. Add the diced potatoes, carrot, and bell pepper to the pot, and continue to simmer for another 20-30 minutes, or until the vegetables are cooked through.
6. If using, stir in the red wine and let the soup simmer for an additional 10 minutes to allow the flavors to meld together.
7. Taste and adjust the seasoning with salt and pepper if needed. Remove the bay leaf before serving.
8. Ladle the Gulaschsuppe into bowls and garnish with chopped fresh parsley.
9. Serve the Gulaschsuppe with slices of rye bread on the side for dipping and sopping up the delicious broth.
10. Enjoy your hearty and comforting Gulaschsuppe with rye bread, perfect for a cozy dinner or lunch on a chilly day!

This Gulaschsuppe recipe is packed with tender beef, hearty vegetables, and aromatic spices, making it a satisfying and flavorful meal. The slices of rye bread are the perfect accompaniment for soaking up the rich and savory broth.

Käsespätzle with Salad

Ingredients:

For the Käsespätzle:

- 2 cups all-purpose flour
- 4 eggs
- 1/2 cup milk
- 1/2 teaspoon salt
- 1/4 teaspoon freshly ground nutmeg
- 3 tablespoons butter
- 2 onions, thinly sliced
- 2 cups shredded Emmental cheese (or any other Swiss cheese)
- Salt and pepper to taste

For the Salad:

- Mixed greens (such as lettuce, spinach, or arugula)
- Cherry tomatoes, halved
- Cucumber, thinly sliced
- Red onion, thinly sliced
- Balsamic vinaigrette or your favorite dressing

Instructions:

1. To make the Käsespätzle, start by preparing the spätzle dough. In a large mixing bowl, combine the flour, eggs, milk, salt, and nutmeg. Mix until a smooth batter forms. Let the batter rest for about 15-20 minutes.
2. While the batter is resting, bring a large pot of salted water to a boil. Once boiling, reduce the heat to a gentle simmer.
3. To form the spätzle, you can either use a spätzle maker or a colander with large holes. Hold the spätzle maker or colander over the pot of simmering water and pour a portion of the batter onto it. Use a spatula to press the batter through the holes, allowing it to drop into the water. Cook the spätzle for about 2-3 minutes, or until they float to the surface. Remove them with a slotted spoon and transfer

them to a colander to drain. Repeat this process until all of the batter has been used.
4. Preheat your oven to 350°F (175°C). In a large skillet, melt 2 tablespoons of butter over medium heat. Add the sliced onions and cook, stirring occasionally, until caramelized and golden brown, about 15-20 minutes. Remove the onions from the skillet and set aside.
5. In the same skillet, add the cooked spätzle and remaining tablespoon of butter. Cook, stirring occasionally, until the spätzle are heated through and starting to turn golden brown.
6. Transfer half of the cooked spätzle to a baking dish. Sprinkle half of the shredded cheese and caramelized onions over the spätzle. Layer the remaining spätzle on top, followed by the remaining cheese and caramelized onions.
7. Bake the Käsespätzle in the preheated oven for about 10-15 minutes, or until the cheese is melted and bubbly.
8. While the Käsespätzle is baking, prepare the salad. In a large bowl, toss together the mixed greens, cherry tomatoes, cucumber, and red onion. Drizzle with balsamic vinaigrette or your favorite dressing, and toss to coat.
9. Once the Käsespätzle is done baking, remove it from the oven and let it cool slightly before serving.
10. Serve the warm Käsespätzle alongside the fresh salad.
11. Enjoy your delicious Käsespätzle with salad, a comforting and satisfying German meal!

This dish is perfect for lunch or dinner and is sure to be a hit with family and friends.

The creamy melted cheese, tender spätzle, and sweet caramelized onions pair

beautifully with the crisp and refreshing salad.

Himmel und Erde (Heaven and Earth) with Blood Sausage

Ingredients:

For the Himmel und Erde:

- 4 large potatoes, peeled and diced
- 2 apples, peeled, cored, and diced
- 1 onion, diced
- 4 slices of blood sausage (Blutwurst)
- 4 tablespoons butter
- Salt and pepper to taste
- Chopped fresh parsley for garnish (optional)

Instructions:

1. Start by boiling the diced potatoes in a pot of salted water until tender, about 10-15 minutes. Drain the potatoes and set them aside.
2. In a large skillet, melt 2 tablespoons of butter over medium heat. Add the diced onion and cook until softened and translucent, about 5 minutes.
3. Add the diced apples to the skillet with the onions and cook until they start to soften, about 3-4 minutes.
4. Add the cooked potatoes to the skillet with the apples and onions. Mash everything together using a potato masher or fork, combining the ingredients well. Season with salt and pepper to taste.
5. In a separate skillet, heat the remaining 2 tablespoons of butter over medium heat. Add the slices of blood sausage and cook until heated through and browned on both sides, about 3-4 minutes per side.
6. To serve, divide the Himmel und Erde mixture onto plates. Top each portion with a slice of blood sausage.
7. Garnish with chopped fresh parsley if desired.
8. Serve the Himmel und Erde with blood sausage immediately, while still warm.
9. Enjoy this hearty and comforting German dish, where the earthiness of the potatoes combines perfectly with the sweetness of the apples, complemented by the rich flavor of the blood sausage.

This dish is perfect for a cozy dinner on a cold evening, and its unique combination of flavors is sure to delight your taste buds!

www.ingramcontent.com/pod-product-compliance
Lightning Source LLC
LaVergne TN
LVHW061943070526
838199LV00060B/3946